IMAGES
of America

AROUND
ELLSWORTH
AND
BLUE HILL

All routes appear to converge in the city of Ellsworth, the gateway to Downeast Maine, in this detail of a 1939 highway map.

IMAGES
of America

AROUND
ELLSWORTH
AND
BLUE HILL

Richard R. Shaw

ARCADIA
PUBLISHING

GREETINGS FROM ELLSWORTH MAINE "the friendly city"

Contents

The graceful bell tower of the First Congregational Church, designed in 1846 by the prominent local architect Thomas Lord, overlooks the Ellsworth City Hall which was completed two years after the Great Fire of 1933 destroyed the former municipal offices.

Introduction

Where I come from, a good way to start an argument is to mention that you're traveling "Downeast," then sit back and ask your friends where they think you're going. Any *real* Mainer will probably say it's Washington County, beyond the city of Ellsworth (which doesn't quite count, even though it's nicknamed the "Gateway to Downeast Maine"). Most tourists will tell you it's ALL of Maine, and a slice of the Canadian Maritime Provinces, to boot. Others will swear it's all of Hancock County, of which Ellsworth is the county seat, with Washington County tossed in.

I weigh in with the faction that thinks "Downeast" is a pleasant state of mind, not a geographical location. That qualifies all of the mid-coastal locales shown in these pages. There are picture book towns like Blue Hill, where the summers are fine and the pace manageable. Or Hancock Point, a half hour's drive away, where the seasonal residents and the locals have co-existed for more than a century. Or, Ellsworth itself, Hancock County's only city, which despite its hustle-bustle traffic that wends its way through to Bar Harbor and points east, retains a homespun flavor that makes it a choice place to visit, and live.

With this book in mind, I used history-rich Ellsworth and Blue Hill as coordinates and set about the task of locating some two hundred good, clear historical photographs that picture life not only in those places, but in the web of towns and hamlets around, and between. This was a crash course, if you will, in modern coastal history that dates back to the eighteenth century, when Blue Hill (1762) was settled by Joseph Wood and John Roundy, and Ellsworth (1763) by Benjamin Milliken. These were the touchstones of later civilization that grew as a result of a closeness to the sea, the Union River, innumerable streams and brooks, pasture land, and blueberry barrens. Not to mention scenic vistas that still can steal your breath.

I knocked on the doors of historians, librarians, collectors, and just plain folks—often they were one in the same—and was heartened that no one ordered this out-of-towner to leave. By project's end, I had gathered hundreds of penny postcards, portraits, maps, glass slides, and ephemera. Then the difficult winnowing process began of selecting pertinent pictures for five chapters.

As with my previous book in this series on my hometown of Bangor, I vowed that this volume would only show what is true. No whitewashing of local history here. There are both mansions and hovels, princes and paupers, and lots of things in between. Even the photograph on p. 64 of the Austin Castle in North Hancock is accompanied by a picture of its plain-looking resident clad simply in housedress and country apron.

A surprising number of the photographs in this book, dating from the 1850s to the 1990s, show women. Men often dominate regional histories but not this one. Maybe because females strove to become equal partners to fishermen, farmers, sailors—or whomever—their visages turned up frequently. Some were far ahead of their time, like the Blue Hill writers-educators Mary Ellen Chase (p. 113) and Esther Wood (p. 112). So were the players on the 1910 girls' basketball team at George Stevens Academy (p. 117), and the telephone operators (p. 87) making do with archaic equipment after the Great Fire of 1933 reduced downtown Ellsworth, phone lines and all, to a pile of ashes.

Because a photograph truly is worth a thousand words, I have, wherever possible, kept the captions brief. The narrative is in the description, but the real story is in the faces of people such as William Howard Taft (p. 81), lovingly captured during a Maine holiday by local photographer Embert Osgood. Dramatic photographs like the one on p. 90 show cresting flood waters laying waste to valuable Ellsworth property in 1923.

I included the chapter, "Transportation: Getting Here from There," because the schooners and steam trains and stagecoaches and airplanes made Hancock County the hub of activity that it is today. Maine Central Railroad tracks linked Ellsworth and Hancock Point to the wonders of Mount Desert Island; coastal steamers ferried travelers across Penobscot Bay from Rockland so they could live their lives, if only for a season, in Blue Hill. Getting around the county has always been extremely important, if a bit challenging. If you've ever driven its serpentine roads you'll know what I mean.

Hopefully, the sincerity of the area's people and its immense natural and manmade beauty reflected in this book, not to mention the rich history, will leave you wanting to visit the region, if you haven't already. Like the boy shown playing the fiddle on the book cover, it is a place filled with the music of nature and that of gifted musicians who find inspiration in the ever-changing seasons, and in the movement of the sea.

Richard R. Shaw
Bangor, Maine

One

Summertime: Season in the Sun

The Sven Gunderson family personifies the fine "summer people" who return each year to Hancock Point. In this photograph from the late 1940s, Dr. Gunderson, a nationally recognized physician, shares a blanket with, from left to right, his daughters Karen (who grew up to marry lyricist Alan Jay Lerner) and Pam (who became the mayor of Lexington, Kentucky), and his wife Harriet (Adams).

Harriet Gunderson (left) and Charlotte Mahon share a boat and conversation off Hancock Point. Both were prominent New England women, contemporaries from Vassar, and lifelong friends. Mrs. Mahon was one of the first delegates to the United Nations.

Bathing at the Big Rock in Blue Hill Bay, captured in this c. 1915 view, has long attracted local residents, as well as visitors anxious to experience Maine's brief but brilliant summertime at the landmark while avoiding the bay's rocky, muddy bottom.

Swimmers swear the water at Lamoine is the coldest of any beach on the East Coast. Perhaps these bathers, photographed near the long pier in 1926, spent more time on the shore than in the Atlantic.

Wives of laborers of the Bangor Gas Light Company enjoy a picnic at Lamoine Beach. The former U.S. Naval Coaling Station (see p. 63) is now the Lamoine State Park.

The Parker Point Wharf, c. 1910, was a short walk or carriage ride to the shops and inns of Blue Hill's Main Street. Steamboats on the Blue Hill Line ferried passengers across the bay from Rockland, making regular stops at Dark Harbor, Eggemoggin, South Brooksville, Brooklin, South Blue Hill, Blue Hill, Surry, and Ellsworth.

This woman and girl appear to be dressed for church, not a hike up Blue Hill Mountain (elevation 940 feet). The summit affords a breathtaking view of rugged Mount Desert Island.

Many cottages built in Maine during the late nineteenth century were designed in the shingled style created by architect William R. Emerson. This angular cottage in Blue Hill still was graceful and functional, a comfortable home to the couple posing by its front porch.

"Wild Rose," later named "Shoreacre," was the first summer cottage built on fashionable Parker Point in Blue Hill. The cottage was completed in 1885 for Fordyce Rogers of Detroit, a paint company president and summer "rusticator" who was given the acre of land the cottage sits on by Hartford Sweet. Rogers painted the dwelling in eight different colors, adding a red roof.

The home and gardens of Ethelbert Woodbridge Nevin (1862–1901) were the pride of Blue Hill Falls, where the Pennsylvania-born composer and his wife spent their summers. His neighbor on nearby Parker Point was fellow musician, Dr. Franz Kneisel (see p. 23), who treated visitors to his property once a year with chamber concerts.

Young students of Miss Adelaide Pearson's art class sketch a cow on the back lawn of the Rowantrees Studio in Blue Hill, in the early 1930s. Miss Pearson started the summer school c. 1930 at her part-time home on Union Street. The only charge was a fee of $1 for each day a student did *not* attend (see pp. 106–108).

George Merchant teaches young Martha Cluveris the finer points of sailing, photographed off Hancock Point *c.* 1912. Merchant is shown later in his life on p. 16.

Waiting for the train at Green Lake, *c.* 1900. Day visitors could disembark a Maine Central Railroad coach at two lakeside stations: one near Nicolin Beach (see p. 65), the other at Jenkins Beach.

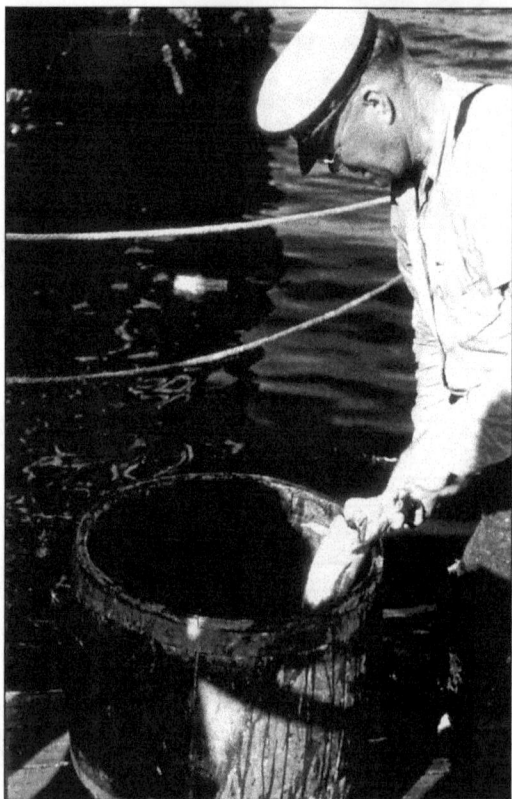

George Lunt began selling lobsters in the 1930s out of his Model T Ford near his property in Trenton. Soon he was required to buy a license and construct a building large enough to hold a pair of scales. Lunt's pound grew along with the price of lobster, regularly serving the Ford and Rockefeller families.

George Merchant inspects a bait barrel in Hancock. In addition to fisherman, Merchant wore the hat of harbor master and builder of lobster boats and fine sailboats.

The tall boilers of Lunt's Lobster Pound, not far from the Thompson Island Bridge in Trenton, have been a landmark for generations, along with the nearby Oak Point Lobster Pound. Sadie Lunt, George's wife, is shown by the fireplaces in the late 1940s. The business was later sold to the Dunbar family.

The Delft (or Delph) Tea Room catered to tourists who summered in Blue Hill. The business, shown here *c.* 1915, was located on the south side of Mill Brook on Main Street.

The tea room's spartan interior suited visitors just fine. Ostentation was for the big city, not quiet, little Blue Hill.

Henry Fonda and Joseph Cotton both acted at the Surry Playhouse, but it was character actor Edward Everett Horton playing the title role in *Springtime for Henry* that remains fixed in many memories. The summer theater, housed in a barn near Contention Cove, was managed by actor Sheppherd Strudwick and operated from the 1920s to the early 1950s.

Snack time at the White Birches Golf Course, located on Route 1 in Hancock. Georgia Raymond (left) and her husband John transformed the old White Birches cabins property into a 53-acre, 9-hole golf course. Georgia's mother, Iva MacCrae, looks on from behind the counter. Doug Smith and George Ray sport beards to mark Ellsworth's Bicentennial in 1963.

Livestock judging at the Blue Hill Fair, for many years a Labor Day weekend tradition, is a complicated study of an animal's proportion, height, and weight. Contestant No. 17 took home a Blue Ribbon in the dairy show, c. 1960, for raising this cow.

The origins of the Blue Hill Fair can be traced back as early as 1878, when a Farmer's Club began meeting at Tucker's Field in Blue Hill Village. But today's mix of agriculture and entertainment was born in 1891 when the first shares in the newly formed Blue Hill Fair Association were sold. The following year the event was moved to the fairgrounds, where it has been held every year since, with the exception of the war year 1944.

When Doris Hodgkins of Hancock married the famous conductor Pierre Monteux, summers in her hometown were never the same. Chamber concerts and musical studies at the Domaine School, started by the couple in 1942, brought many musicians and visitors to the village. In this portrait, Doris (third from left) is pictured as a young woman with, from left to right, Hilda Davis (her sister), Bertha Hodgkins (her mother), and Charlotte Michlin (her other sister).

Pierre and Doris Monteux at their "Camp Paradise" in Hancock in 1943. The brilliant French conductor became a U.S. citizen in 1942 and used his Hancock home for rest and relaxation between conducting engagements around the world.

Musicians of Blue Hill's summer colony have held weekly concerts in Kneisel Hall for many years. This was formerly the hillside studio of Dr. Franz Kneisel (1865–1926), a Romanian violinist who was concert-master of the Boston Symphony Orchestra and founder of the esteemed Kneisel chamber music quartet.

Joseph Fuchs was a young violinist from New York when he began summer studies with Dr. Kneisel. Fuchs returned to Blue Hill to perform long after Kneisel's death, as did his sister Lillian, who played the viola.

Many a summer night filled with laughter and romance was spent at the Ellsworth-Trenton Drive-In, the first (and only) outdoor theater in Hancock County. After opening in 1952, one loud speaker broke the night's serenity, but later individual car speakers were installed for privacy and improved sound quality.

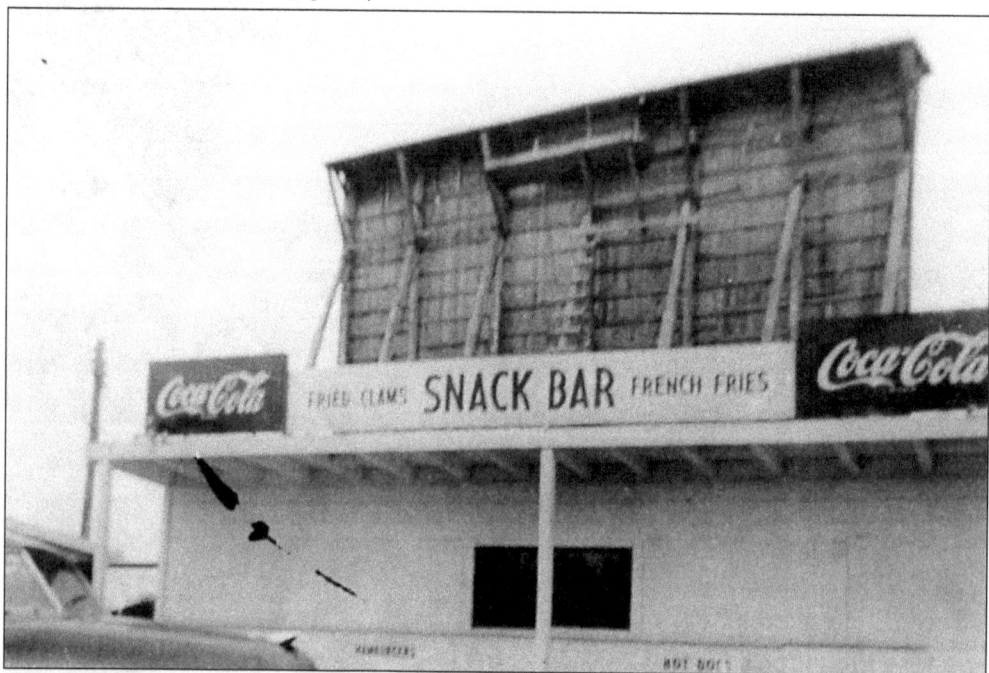

The Ellsworth-Trenton Drive-In sold fried clams and french fries along with theater tickets. Patrons drove the short distance from Bar Harbor, and from throughout Hancock County. Sam Nyer closed the business in 1986, the victim of competition from home video and an indoor theater at an Ellsworth shopping center.

Camp Jordan on Branch Lake in Ellsworth has been operated by the Bangor YMCA for many years. This photograph, taken in 1960, pictures a newly dedicated cabin, donated by the Bangor-Brewer Lions Club. From left to right are Chuck Marquez (camp counselor), Eugene Syphers (camper), Charles Roberts (acting King Lion), Mike Oliver (counselor), and Thomas Emery (camper).

Willie Shubert offers pointers on building a campfire at Camp Jordan in April 1961. The summer camp began for boys only, but later was made co-educational.

Francis Hamabe, a gifted artist who has been summering in Blue Hill since 1950, titled this silkscreen print *Kayaks at the Blue Hill Falls*. Hamabe's studio is located on tiny Mill Island

overlooking the falls. Kayakers return each year to experience the rush of the tidal falls, which backs up into a salt pond.

The old double-decked grandstand at Wyman Park in Ellsworth, seen here in the 1890s, and a later single-story structure (built c. 1923 after the original one burned) seated crowds that converged on the fairground to watch boxing matches, orchestra concerts, and fair activities. Herbert T. Silbsy II recalled watching a solar eclipse through smoked glasses at the 1934 Ellsworth Fair, its final year of operation.

Two

Transportation: Getting Here from There

The steamer *Catherine* was the special pride of Captain Oscar A. Crockett, the father of the Blue Hill Lines, who had her built in Bath in 1893. The 161-ton ferry never had an accident, the closest being the day she briefly was hung up on a ledge.

Can you imagine riding this Concord-style stagecoach a century ago, on the 120-mile route from Ellsworth to Calais? There were no springs, only a body slung onto leather straps over a wooden frame that jostled passengers back and forth. Attempting to thwart the business of a competing stage line from Bangor to Calais, on the rugged (but shorter) "Airline" Road, the coach operator on the longer route published a fictitious portrayal of wolves attacking the Airline stage. The ploy backfired when paying passengers showed up armed with shotguns, hoping to shoot wolves on the Airline.

The road from Ellsworth Falls, where there were once five sawmills, to the town wharves on the east side of the Union River was thick with mud when this late nineteenth century view was taken. Downtown shoppers complained that they couldn't cross Main Street because of the endless lumber traffic.

Ross Taylor operated the Contention Cove Express, which carried "summer people" from the railroad station in Ellsworth to the cove in Surry, where they boarded steamers that crossed the bay to Rockland. This was a lightweight version of the Concord coach pictured on p. 30.

Maine Central Railroad day coaches sit idle at Mount Desert Ferry in Hancock Point, where passengers could travel the 8 miles across Frenchman Bay to Bar Harbor. An 1899 ferry tragedy, in which twenty-one were drowned and scores injured when a ferry slip collapsed, occurred to the right of the small building near the center. A three-masted schooner, or "coaster," is visible in the bay.

Granite ships such as this were occasionally blown aground in Hancock trying to negotiate the tricky tidal falls of the lower Taunton River. Ships loaded with tons of stone had to sail precisely on the tide, or disaster could be the result.

Because of its speed, this two-masted schooner, built in Ellsworth in 1870, was named the *Storm Petrel* (after a small, dark sea bird with long wings). Coasters like this were good working boats, carrying general freight along the New England coast and beyond. Many fine schooners were built on the Union River during this period.

The fluted smokestack of the steamer *Senator* resembled the stacks on Mississippi River steamboats. Built in Ellsworth and hauled over land by horses, the vessel ran excursions on Green Lake in the 1890s. Buffalo Bill Cote is fabled to have boarded the craft while en route by train to a circus performance in Ellsworth.

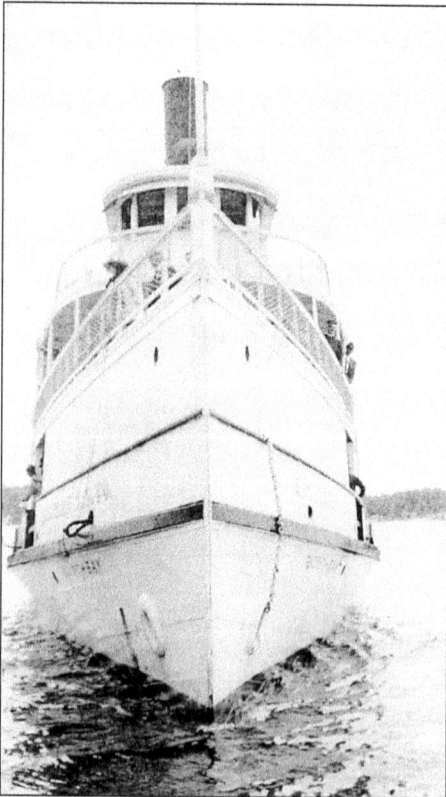

When the *Boothbay* steamed into Blue Hill, residents would gawk at the awkward-looking, iron-hulled craft with the tall smokestack and wonder how it stayed afloat. She performed extremely well on the water, however, and had a huge freight capacity. With the demise of Blue Hill's steam era, she saw service in 1939 in New York, where she ferried tourists to the Statue of Liberty.

A deckhand with the Maine Central Railroad steamer *Rangeley* wears a visor cap with gold braid, a black sweater with the title of his boat across the chest, and dark trousers.

Built in 1913 in Bath, the *Rangeley* provided regularly scheduled service to Mount Desert Ferry at Hancock Point. She was the last of Maine Central's fine fleet of steamboats, and in 1925 was moved to the Hudson River, after falling victim to World War I conditions and competition from the automobile.

Steamboat travel was prone to mishaps. The Maine Central steamer *Norumbega* ran out of Mount Desert Ferry for more than twenty years without incident. Then one day she ran aground off Clark's Point near Mount Desert Island when a problem with accumulated steam developed. Fortunately, the boat was undamaged, no one was injured, and the boat was nudged on its way by a tugboat.

A rare view from the water shows the wharf at Hancock Point in 1908. The Bluffs Hotel, built by the Maine Central Railroad in 1885, towers over the scene with its more than one hundred guest rooms.

Frenchman's Bay
Steamboat Line.

ALL THE YEAR ROUND!

STEAMER

Electa,

Capt. E. TRUE,

Runs to the various ports in Frenchman's Bay Every Week Day in Connection with the

MAINE CENTRAL R. R.

Summer Arrangement.

Leave Hancock at 5.00 A. M.; Sullivan at 5.45 A. M. for Mount Desert Ferry,

Connecting with the Morning Train for

BANGOR, PORTLAND & BOSTON.

Leave Mount Desert Ferry, for Sullivan,

On arrival of the morning train from the West; Leave Sullivan for Bar Harbor at 9.10, Hancock 9.40, Lamoine 10.15 arriving at Bar Harbor 11.10 A. M.

Leave Bar Harbor for Winter Harbor

At 11.45 A. M.

— RETURNING. —

Leave Winter Harbor

At 12.45, Bar Harbor 2.00, Lamoine 2.45, Hancock 3.25, Sullivan 4.10 P. M., arriving at Mount Desert Ferry in season to connect with night train for Bangor, Portland and Boston.

Leaves Mount Desert Ferry

On arrival of the night train from the West, for Sullivan and Hancock.

The Frenchman's Bay Steamboat Line did a brisk business east of Bar Harbor. The 64-foot *Electa* was built in Brewer in 1892 and for twenty years ran out of Bangor, Belfast, and Rockland in addition to serving Hancock County.

Henry Billings shows off Ellsworth's first wheelbarrow express. This photograph was taken long before the Great 1933 Fire leveled Harvey and Fred Morang's confectionary store, visible behind Billings. The Webster House (far left), a non-transient hotel, burned some thirty-five years after the Great Fire.

Ferry service between Sullivan and Hancock continued into the 1930s, even after the completion of the iron bridge connected those towns in 1923 (see p. 67). This view shows the ferry docking at Sullivan, near the site of the present bridge. The tolls were 10¢ for a special trip, 5¢ if one was waiting for the train to arrive at nearby Waukeag station.

The *Little Round Top* was a 23-ton steam tug out of Ellsworth. Built in 1871, she was owned by Henry M. Hall and others in 1875, and later by Haynes and Whitney Company. The boat could tow two or three schooners at a time up the Union River, pushing aside any sawmill slabs and sawdust that lay in her path.

This primitive delivery vehicle, parked in front of the Hancock House in Ellsworth *c.* 1922, wasn't too far removed from a horse-drawn wagon. Note the pneumatic tires with winter chains.

An old-fashioned crossing gate rises above the Maine Central Railroad station in Ellsworth, c. 1912. The station was once a beehive of activity, especially in the summer, when limousines were driven from Bar Harbor to pick up wealthy residents. The station was demolished in 1928, and the present brick station, now owned by the Bangor Hydro-Electric Company, built in its place.

This dramatic photograph was taken not long after the Maine Central Railroad Company built its tracks through Ellsworth to Washington Junction in 1886. Probably taken off High Street, looking north, it shows a diamond-shaped smokestack on a coal-burning locomotive, inside of which were screens and baffles to prevent cinders from burning up the countryside.

When President Benjamin Harrison arrived at Mount Desert Ferry aboard the Bar Harbor Express in August 1889, spectators saw a locomotive festooned with ribbons and bunting. The man in the portrait mounted on the front of the engine is probably Hannibal Hamlin, then the nation's only living ex-vice president and a summer resident of Hancock Point.

Maine Central Railroad car cleaners were kept busy at Mount Desert Ferry, where several trains arrived daily. They are, from left to right, Everard Grant, Cal Martin, Frank Murphy, Ellen Murphy, Mr. Goldsberry, Leola Black, and Archie Gatcomb.

The Pontiac dealership on High Street in Ellsworth in 1937. All of the cars on display are brand new Pontiacs. Fred Silvy and John Kief operated the business, later named Dow Pontiac. The man holding the gasoline hose is Arnold Lee. An Irving station eventually replaced the dealership.

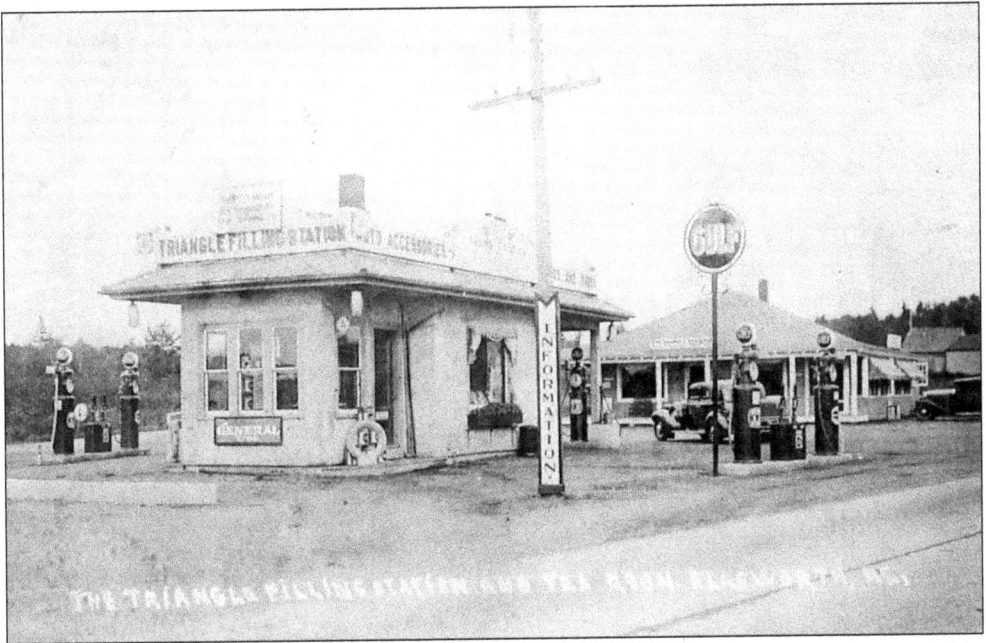

The Triangle Filling Station and Tea Room, now the site of Linnehan's Ellsworth Ford Sales, was a landmark at the Triangle (the junction of Routes 1 and 3). Medbra Cousins ran the business in the 1930s, when this view was taken. The concrete road, completed in 1926 (see p. 45), increased traffic flow into the area.

A busy day at the Blue Hill Fair in the 1920s. Among the classic automobiles parked in back of the trotting track is a Model T Ford in the lower right.

The Bar Harbor Airport in Trenton is shown here in 1989 with jets and propeller-driven airplanes on the tarmac. Work on the airport began during the Great Depression when it was partially funded by the Work Projects Administration.

Harry Parker, an Ellsworth bank teller, designed and built this rear-engined, streamlined, four-passenger sedan in his spare time, c. 1930, using the parts of seventeen cars. It could reach a top speed of 103 mph, got 23 miles to the gallon, and slept 2 people.

"Going down the cement" was a common term in the 1920s and 1930s, after this veritable superhighway of 40-foot concrete slabs was laid in Ellsworth and Trenton. Started in 1926 and completed a year later, it replaced an inferior dirt highway like the one pictured below.

Around the 1890s, a boy with a bicycle chats with a man in a carriage on the narrow ribbon of road that would eventually become U.S. Route 1 in Hancock.

Balloon ascensions were front page news in the 1890s, when this dramatic photograph was taken in Hancock County. Inflating the balloon could last for hours, and when—and if—the balloonist became airborne, he was at the whim of the winds. Once, a Bangor ascension went awry when the balloonist ended up miles away, near Chick Hill in Clifton.

Three
Landmarks:
Natural and Manmade

The Black Mansion in Ellsworth was the home of Colonel John Black, agent for William Bingham, who owned large tracts of land east of the Penobscot River. In 1900, long after John had died, his grandson, George Nixon Black, hired photographer Embert Osgood to photograph his house from the level of the first floor on a specially built platform resting on the rapidly sloping hill. No other picture like it exists.

Colonel Black's home, built *c.* 1826, is restored to its original appearance. Lining the walls of the lovely curving staircase are several oil portraits, the largest of which pictures Black's father-in-law, General David Cobb, the first agent in Maine for the Bingham Estate.

The old kitchen of the Black Mansion is just as Black would remember it, complete with a pair of moose antlers hanging above the fireplace.

An unusual winter scene of the elegant brick structure shows snow hanging heavy on the trees. A curious feature of the home is that it has no front door—visitors must enter from the side. Maybe Black wanted only windows on the front to admire the sweeping view to the south.

Colonel John Black (1781–1856) was a driving personality who became the richest man east of Bangor at a time when land speculation could make or break a man. Black took many chances, and won nearly all of them.

The Blue Hill Inn stood at the crest of Tenney Hill from 1892, when it was built by George Stover, to 1932, the year it was destroyed by fire. Vacationers could enjoy sailboat excursions down the bay, arranged by hotel staff, and buckboard rides to Castine and other points in the county. An orchestra played each Saturday night, an occasion for young townspeople to join the guests.

The printed message on the back of this 1913 postcard view reads, "Hancock House, home to those who visit Down East, in the heart of Maine's hunting, fishing, summer and winter sports. Old fashioned hospitality prevails in Dining Room and Cocktail Lounge. Delightful rooms with bath." The Ellsworth landmark stood just across the bridge on the west side of town.

This homey-looking hotel, which dated back to 1836, was located on the present site of the Ellsworth Post Office. According to local legend, the hotel was demolished in 1918, and the lumber shipped to Europe to build trenches in the waning months of World War I. Others insist they saw it as late as 1920, and that the wood was used for construction of local buildings.

Blue Hill Mountain is one of Hancock County's most visible natural landmarks. Seen here from the site of the present Parker Point Road golf course, the mountain got its name from early sailors and others who remarked on its bluish hue.

The Blue Hill Memorial Hospital on Water Street, now much expanded and modernized, was a modest operation when this view was postmarked in 1951. Senior townspeople still refer to the old home as the Bliss House, after Dr. R.N.V. Bliss, a long-time supervisor.

52

With the help of his parishioners, Reverend Jonathan Fisher (1768–1847) built this simple wooden home after he moved to Blue Hill in 1796. The Harvard-educated poet, painter, farmer, and first parson of the local Congregational Church, made the paint for his home from yellow ocher he discovered nearby.

Fisher was never predictable, as evidenced by his curious self-profile surrounded by trees and wild animals. This and other wood engravings illustrated his book *Scripture Animals or Natural History of the Living Creatures Named in the Bible, Written Especially For Youth*.

Union Street, the "road to Orland," was lined with graceful old homes and trees when this view was taken c. 1912. Dutch Elm Disease has claimed many elms in the past thirty years. Their future in towns such as Blue Hill is bleak.

Remove the old vehicles and several of the elm trees from this view of Blue Hill in the early 1930s and it could have been taken today. Main Street is graced by fine old homes and businesses that seem frozen in time. Charlie Wescott's blacksmith shop (far right) has been transformed into the Firepond Restaurant.

The Blue Hill House, now named the Blue Hill Inn, was built c. 1830 as a private residence by a blacksmith named Edward Varnum Stevens. He had already converted the place to an inn when he sold it to Haskell Hinckley, whose wife Fannie operated the place for many years, once estimating she had accommodated 50,000 guests.

Pendleton..

House,

Leach Brothers,
Proprietors.

Newly Furnished.
Steam Heat.
Baths.

First=Class Livery.   Long Distance Telephone.   Bluehill, Maine.

One of Blue Hill's premier landmarks still stands near the center of town. Although the Pendleton House hasn't been a hotel since 1912, the name has stuck. Built prior to 1832 by Jeremiah T. Holt, the building was purchased by Nathan P. Pendleton of Boston in 1878 and later was leased by Eugene Leach and his brother.

Maine Governor John H. Reed helped plant a chestnut tree at the village blacksmith shop in Blue Hill in 1960. Others at the ceremony were, from left to right, Katherine Austin (shop owner), Mrs. Charles Wescott (widow of the former owner), and Elizabeth Wescott (her daughter). The tree still grows on the Main Street property, reminding passersby of the classic poem by Maine's Henry Wadsworth Longfellow, *The Village Blacksmith*, and its mention of the "spreading chestnut tree."

This unique fence with a rosette gate, the only such fence to survive in town, borders the Holt House, now the home of the Blue Hill Historical Society. The early home, with its kitchen fireplace and stenciled walls, was built in 1815 by Jeremiah Thorndike Holt, the grandson of Nicholas Holt. Nicholas brought his family from Andover, Massachusetts, in 1765; they were the fifth family to arrive in town.

They don't make doorways like this anymore. The Elms, located on Main Street and long known as the John Stevens House, was built in 1832 by Hosea Kittredge, a preceptor of Blue Hill Academy and the husband of Nancy Fisher (daughter of Parson Jonathan Fisher). The front porch was added in 1900.

The Blue Hill Academy was located in this building from 1833, when it was opened, to 1898, when a new academy building was constructed on the property of George Stevens. Stevens, a businessman and devout Baptist, left most of his estate in his will to a board of trustees who incorporated the school in his name. Today, the George Stevens Academy is one of the most respected schools in Maine.

Silver, copper, and gold were all mined with mixed success in Blue Hill beginning as early as the mining boom of the 1870s, but granite quarrying was in a class by itself. This granite works, located off the East Blue Hill Road, c. 1910, shows the long cutting sheds which gave workers protection in inclement weather.

E.C. Williams' repair shop was a busy Blue Hill business at a time when a well-maintained pair of boots or shoes could last a lifetime. An empty hay wagon sits idle in Williams' backyard, and in his shop window a broadside announces an upcoming Democratic rally.

Since its earliest years in the late eighteenth century, Blue Hill has prided itself on being a literate community. The proof is in this handsome library building, opened in 1940 with the help of Miss Adelaide Pearson (see p. 108), who solicited private donations, and Anne Hinckley, who secured aid from the Public Works Administration.

Who would believe these companion buildings were actually built eighty-nine years? The First Congregational Church (1846) is one of the prettiest churches in Maine, and the Ellsworth City Hall (1935), with its Scandinavian design, is a handsome municipal building.

The minister preached from a high pulpit and parishioners sat in box pews after the Blue Hill Baptist Church was built in 1817. Thomas Lord remodeled the interior of the church to its present appearance in the 1850s.

Blue Hill's Congregational Church replaced an earlier church that burned to the ground in 1842. Thomas Lord, who built fourteen church buildings in Hancock County, oversaw construction of this one, which was dedicated in January 1843. The bell is a recasting of the Paul Revere bell which was destroyed in the 1842 meetinghouse fire.

The North Penobscot United Methodist Church graced the high ground at the intersection of Routes 15 and 199 for 150 years. In 1991 it was dismantled and moved down the hill to Blue Hill, where it was resurrected as the new home of the St. Francis-by-the-Sea Episcopal Church on Route 177.

Bluehill Bay, Me. Sand Island Light.

In 1995 the former 1857 Blue Hill Light Station on what is now called Green Island, off of Brooklin, was put on the real estate market. Prospective buyers were informed that the tiny island's size fluctuates with the tide.

BATTLE OF NASKEAG

The Battle of Naskeag was no Lexington or Bunker Hill, but historians argue its relative importance in local history. In July 1778, William Reed, working in a field near the shore, saw a British sloop approaching with a party of sixty men. Fellow townsmen opened fire, killing two of the enemy. The British were able to burn some buildings and capture some livestock, which they returned the next day when they came back on shore under a flag of truce and fled with several of their captured soldiers.

The Crabtree Neck Lighthouse off Hancock Point was cut up and sold for scrap during World War II. The *Norumbega* (see p. 36) is steaming across the bay in the background, while the three-masted schooner *Winchester* sails in the foreground.

The U.S. Naval Coaling Station at Lamoine was built after the Spanish-American War. Freight ships hauled coal to Maine from Norfolk, Virginia; here, the coal is being loaded onto Navy ships. A good deal of politics went into building the multi-million-dollar project: Eugene Hale of Ellsworth was one of the nation's most influential senators, and former Senator James G. Blaine had a summer home at Bar Harbor.

Miss Neva Ethel Austin and her sister Altea led reclusive lives in what came to be known as Austin Castle in North Hancock. The castle was built by their father, Theodore, a wealthy New York jeweler, who moved to Maine in 1870.

Mr. and Mrs. Austin died soon after building this 40-room estate of wood, stained glass, and fine fieldstone, leaving their two daughters to fend for themselves. But Neva and Altea lost much of their inherited wealth during the Great Depression and lived the remainder of their lives in one room of the castle, keeping all the other rooms patrolled twenty-four hours a day.

Nicolin (pronounced Nic-OH-lin, reputedly of Indian origin) is located on Route 1A north of Ellsworth Falls. Just after the turn of the century, when this view was taken, the settlement's only landmarks were the town post office, cemetery, and Grange Hall.

Nicolin Beach on the west side of Green Lake is several miles off Route 1A. A campground there has drawn many Canadian visitors in recent years.

The new Union River Bridge was the talk of Ellsworth at the time this postcard view was made in the 1920s. The Great Flood of 1923 carried away the steel bridge on this site. The Hancock House (right) and the garage buildings on both sides of west Main Street were demolished many years later.

The Union River falls 60 feet over the hydro dam at Ellsworth, the greatest height of any dam in Maine. The engineering wonder still supplies power for the Ellsworth area and all of Mount Desert Island. It is now operated by the Bangor Hydro-Electric Company.

Engineers braved the tricky whirlpools of the Taunton River when they built the pilings of this five-span steel bridge in 1923. Ferry service (see p. 38) connected Sullivan and Hancock before, during, and a few years following the bridge's completion.

Children remarked that the bridge sang when their parents drove over its corrugated floor, hence its nickname "The Singing Bridge." In reality, many Maine bridges "sang," depending on how closely one listened.

One of the earliest daguerreotypes of Ellsworth shows a frontier town ripe for growth. Probably taken between 1850–1855, the view pictures buildings along the Union River, and the muddy hill that was Main Street. The two facing brick blocks (center) are the only buildings standing today.

State Street in 1895 was a study in solid, three-story brick buildings. The newspaper office of *The Ellsworth American* was at the right. At far left was the old post office and custom house, with its revolving door. Across the street, to the right, the GAR Hall occupied the third floor; beneath it, on the second floor, were the offices of Judge John Peters Jr.

The village of Sedgwick hasn't changed significantly in the years since this photograph was taken from across the Benjamin River in Brooklin, *c.* 1860. The 1837 Baptist Church still stands, regarded as one of the handsomest Greek Revival churches ever built, as do some of the dwellings in the foreground.

The Great Fire of 1933 (see Chapter 4) ravaged most of these wooden buildings, shown here in 1895. On the left side of the alley where the inferno began was Luchini's fruit and confectionary

store and a dentist's office. Irving Osgood's photographic studio is also clearly visible. The brick Union Trust Block (far left), at the corner of State and Main Streets, was spared the fire's fury.

Ellsworth, Maine., Public Library.

One of the grand old homes to survive the Great Fire of 1933 was the Tisdale House, since 1897 the home of the Ellsworth Public Library. Colonel Meltiah Jordan built the house in 1817. His son Benjamin lived there until his death, and after that it was occupied by Judge Joshua Hathaway, followed by a house-joiner and shipbuilder named Seth Tisdale. Colonel John Black's grandson, George Nixon Black, bought the property and had it remodeled in 1897, donating it to the town as a public library. An addition was constructed in 1991.

The former Hancock County Courthouse, built in 1886, is remembered for the many legal cases tried there, but also for the fire there in 1929 that killed two firefighters. The old jail (left) houses the collection of the Ellsworth Historical Society.

72

The old hardwood turning mill on State Street was yet another Ellsworth landmark that burned. This one virtually exploded as flames ate the sawdust that had accumulated from years of turning such items as pilasters and mop handles. The mill's construction, c. 1890, was a major economic scheme funded for $100,000 by the Board of Trade.

Hancock Hall, built in 1869, graced upper Main Street until it was destroyed in the 1933 Fire (see p. 86). Ellsworth's town offices were located on the first floor; upstairs was a large hall where politicians spoke, orchestras played, and Victorian-era couples danced the "Grand March" just like Scarlett and Rhett in Gone With the Wind.

Ann Miller, starring in *Reveille with Beverly*, was wowing audiences with her million-dollar legs when this snapshot of the Grand Theater was taken in 1943. Now a performing arts center, the movie house was a hit in Ellsworth after it hawked its first ticket to a Cary Grant-Katharine Hepburn movie in 1937. Harvard Jellison's ice cream parlor was next door.

Smiling children exit the Dirigo Theater on State Street in the 1930s (the site is now the back parking lot of the Union Trust Company). The plain wooden movie house never measured up to the Grand, which truly was grand by Hancock County standards, but no one complained. Tickets and popcorn were cheap, and the movies current.

Xenophon (George) Panos, owner of the Central Cafe on the north side of Main Street, was a Greek immigrant who waited tables, baked pies, and cooked dinners of chicken, steaks, chops, and seafood. Behind the counter with Panos in this c. 1940 photograph are, from left to right, Hester Shackford, Ruth Carlisle, Irene Panos, and Alice Angelieas.

Hollis B. Estey (center), c. 1910, with the family dog and laundry workers. Estey was a genial man who ran a steam laundry on State Street in Ellsworth. Laundries then were hot and steamy places in which to work. Laborers were required to crank the washers by hand. Estey laundered awnings and other heavy goods in addition to everyday clothing.

Day and Night is the title of this striking two-headed sculpture created in recent years by the late Lenore Thomas Straus. Ms. Straus stipulated in her will that the work of art be given to the town of Blue Hill if the Leighton Gallery in that town ceases to exist.

Four

Happenings:
Milestones in Our Lives

The Great Fire of May 7, 1933, reduced most of downtown Ellsworth to a charred ruin. In this view, firemen make a stand on Main Street to prevent the sparks from spreading, a wasted effort since a stiff southerly wind carried burning embers onto the right side of the street, and beyond.

When the village of Surry celebrated the centennial of its incorporation in 1903, a dozen of its adult residents, and one child, posed for this portrait. Nellie Hagerthy read a poem by F.B. Foss that alluded to the blessing of its relative obscurity: "And must we all foresake her/ And turn her down at last/ Because she is not a city/ Filled up with sin and strife . . .?"

Professor Hurd, perhaps a traveling salesman or politician, delivers a soapbox speech in Ellsworth, c. 1895. The location is probably Bridge Hill in front of the old county buildings. Such activity was common there, as well as across the river at the railroad terminal.

Umbrellas protect aged spectators from the sun in 1910 while a speaker stands on the steps of Wakonda, a cottage on Mill Island at Blue Hill Falls, and remarks on the town's first settlers. A tablet in honor of the settlers (see below) was being unveiled that day by the Blue Hill Historical Society.

Men and women arrive on foot and by carriage for the unveiling of the tablet, which noted that Joseph Wood and John Roundy of Beverly, Massachusetts, landed near that spot on April 7, 1762, and built two log cabins. The pioneers returned the following year, each with a wife and six small children.

Downtown Ellsworth was awash with bunting in the 1880s on what was probably the Fourth of July. Wiggin and Moore Druggists was a fixture at the corner of Water and Main Streets well into the twentieth century, operating in later years under the name of Moore's Drugstore.

President William Howard Taft's visit to Ellsworth on July 23, 1910, made national headlines. The chief executive is the centerpiece of this portrait, taken at the home of Senator and Mrs. Eugene Hale. From left to right are: (standing) Assistant Secretary of the Navy Berkman Winthrop, former Maine Governor John Hill, Mrs. Hill, Captain Archie Butts (lost on the Titanic in 1912), Taft's private secretary H.D. Norton, Senator Hale, Mrs. Horace Taft, Miss Boardman, and the President's son Horace Taft; (sitting) Mrs. Hale, Professor Moore, the President, Mrs. Taft (with hat), and Mrs. Taft's sister Mrs. Moore.

A trio of musicians performs in the middle of Main Street in Ellsworth in the 1890s. Street entertainers drummed up business for traveling carnivals and attractions at Hancock Hall by playing music for free. The boys might be brothers, the harpist their father.

An *c.* 1890s pie-eating contest, probably at Wyman Park (the fairgrounds) in Ellsworth. The boy with the fastest gums and heartiest appetite usually won, while under the watchful eye of a judge who inspected the plates when the boys were finished.

Monaghan's Band attracted crowds wherever it played. Here the group pauses at the corner of Oak and Main Streets, c. 1898. Herb Monaghan and his son Paul were gifted local musicians. Note the Unitarian Church building in the background, now the site of a Dunkin' Donuts.

Ellsworth's Bicentennial festivities in 1963 gave local women an opportunity to dress in long, flowing dresses of a bygone era. Ruth Brown (far right) and Norma Beal (second from right) are just two of the "Bowery Belles." Located on Water Street, the Bowery was a raucous riverfront neighborhood.

Hose fights always drew a crowd, such as this one on Main Street, *c.* 1895. Volunteer firefighters drawing water from a hand pumper would aim their hoses vertically or horizontally, occasionally reaching a height of up to 184 feet.

Contestants at the 1963 Ellsworth Bicentennial observance re-enact a hose fight. The city's first muster featuring a local engine was on October 13, 1859. The Senator Hale Hose Company was organized in 1896 after the city bought horse-drawn hose carts, putting the individual hand-drawn pumper teams out of commission.

The burning of Hancock Hall on the evening of May 7, 1933, illustrates the high drama of Ellsworth's worst conflagration. Attempting to save the hall, firefighters dynamited the Partridge house (seen burning to the left of the hall), but they inadvertently set Hancock Hall on fire.

Main Street after the fire was a scene of total devastation. The shell of Hancock Hall stands at the right, and in the distance lies the rubble of many local businesses that had already been stung by the losses of the Great Depression.

The telephone company's central office was relocated to the old Hosea Phillips house at Church and Oak Streets after the main office downtown was burned in the Great 1933 Fire. Telephone service west to Blue Hill was interrupted by the fire since the line ran off of Main Street, where the heaviest damage was inflicted.

Callers exercised patience and restraint while waiting to telephone out of Ellsworth following the Great Fire. Because the main switchboard was no longer functioning, local operators made do with more primitive equipment until service was restored. The operators are, from left to right, Margaret Davis, Phyllis Harrington, Ernestine Shea, and Catherine Morrison.

Only the Webster House (the large white building, across Main Street from the ruins of Hancock Hall) and a few other structures escaped the fury of the Ellsworth Fire. The fire started the evening of May 7, 1933, in an old building behind the north side of Main Street. Eighteen fire departments responded to the emergency calls, but a stiff wind that drove the fire like a

furnace was too fierce a foe to combat effectively. Since President Franklin D. Roosevelt had closed the banks just weeks before, property owners were forced to borrow money on good faith from friends and institutions just to survive.

Ellsworth's other great calamity was the Great Flood of 1923. Flood waters turned the Union River into a rising torrent that took out these old wooden sheds behind the Peters Block on the east bank.

The steel bridge connecting the east and west sides of Ellsworth was also carried away by the flood. The Hancock House and surrounding buildings (visible in the distance), located away from the river's west shore, were not damaged.

Mother Nature acted swiftly after the upper dam, built as a storage facility to create Graham Lake, gave way and flooded the city below. The lower hydro dam in the city held fast.

Losses exceeding $300,000 were recorded after the Great Flood of May 2, 1923. This view looks up the Union River toward the business district. The west side of Ellsworth was left without a water supply, and the entire city had no electricity.

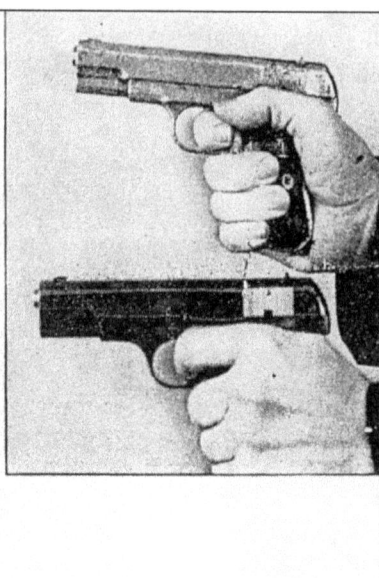

Harvard Hodgkins became a national celebrity after the FBI revealed in January 1945 that he and Mary Forsi, both of Hancock, had contributed to the capture of two Nazi spies who put ashore at Hancock Point on the stormy night of November 29, 1944. Newspapers reported that the Germans each carried a revolver. Hodgkins later met Babe Ruth at his New York apartment.

The clean-cut Hodgkins, seen here at the time of the spy incident, made perfect fodder for newspaper reporters who chronicled activities in the life of the seventeen-year-old Boy Scout.

Two would-be saboteurs from this German U-boat sneaked onto Hancock Point. William Colepaugh and Erich Gimpel were later sentenced to death by hanging, which was later commuted to thirty years in prison. Horst Haslau, radio officer of German U-Boat 1230, returned to Maine in 1987 to look over the coastal area where the spies put ashore. Speaking of periodic reunions of the men pictured here, Haslau remarked, "We're getting along [in years]. Each year there is another one or two missing."

Irving Osgood (center, front), commandant of the William H.H. Rice Post No. 55 of the Grand Army of the Republic, stood before the camera in this c. 1890 photograph, taken at an encampment in Sorrento. Osgood was a prominent Ellsworth photographer, and was wounded at the Battle of Gettysburg. He was one of 653 men the town sent off to fight the Confederate forces.

Memorial Day 1886 was a solemn occasion for these aging veterans from Post No. 55, who fanned across Main Street to have their picture taken. The post was chartered in 1882 and disbanded in 1923. In 1887 it dedicated a Civil War monument before a large crowd on Bridge Hill.

Father John Bapst was a Swiss Jesuit who became the parish priest of the Catholic Church in Ellsworth. Cartoons such as this one, printed in *The Ellsworth American* by publisher William H. Chaney, fanned nativist, anti-Catholic, sentiment. A dispute over the teaching of the King James Bible in the parochial school culminated in an assault on Father John on the evening of October 14, 1854. Nativists stripped him naked, tarred and feathered him, and rode him around town on a board. Disgraced, John left Ellsworth for Bangor, where he became the first rector of St. John's Catholic Church.

Five

People:
Windows onto the Soul

The Meyer Davis family of Hancock enjoys an evening of song around the piano. From left to right are Meyer (a society orchestra leader), daughter Ginia (a soprano), Garry, Meyer Jr., and Emery, with Marjorie at the piano.

This staunch Federalist never set foot in the present city of Ellsworth, but that didn't stop the few residents of New Bowdoin or Township No. 7 from incorporating their town in his name on February 26, 1800. Townspeople shared the political sentiments of Oliver Ellsworth, the third Chief Justice of the United States Supreme Court, as did much of the young nation.

Hannibal Emery Hamlin (1858–1938) was one of Ellsworth's best-known citizens in the many years that he practiced law there. The son and namesake of Abraham Lincoln's first vice president, Hamlin was Maine attorney general, Senate president, and law partner in the firm of Hale, Emery and Hamlin.

At the peak of his career, Eugene Hale (1836–1918) was one of the nation's most influential senators. Small of stature but never lacking in energy, the Ellsworth attorney was a conservative Republican whose love of gourmet cooking was legendary. In 1874 President Grant appointed him postmaster general and in 1911 he retired from the U.S. Senate after thirty years of service.

Linen tablecloths appear out of place in this 1890s-era view of the main lodge at Tunk Lake in Sullivan. But these distinguished looking visitors, probably "from away," were no ordinary guests. Harry Stanwood, the flamboyant younger brother of naturalist Cordelia Stanwood (see pp. 104–105), operated Big Chief's Camps between Big and Little Tunk for many years.

Card players pause to have their picture taken at Big Chief's Camps. Harry Stanwood made extra money by hiring photographers to record the activities of paying guests, who in turn would order copies of their images to pack in their suitcases. Card games such as whist were popular at sporting camps.

Bill Pomroy, a beloved Ellsworth character, was perhaps best known as being the caretaker of the home of Hannibal E. Hamlin, a local attorney (see p. 99). Here he poses with a large goat that studies the camera's lens with much curiosity.

Diego was a trotting stallion owned by F.C. Burrill of the Burrill National Bank (later Liberty National Bank) in Ellsworth. Trotting parks were extremely popular in Maine before the automobile robbed horses of their value to society.

Bill Pomry, the man with the goat on the preceding page, has his hair cut in George Gould's Main Street barber shop. Before the 1933 Fire, Gould's shop was a great place to have a shave and hear the latest gossip. After the fire, Gould moved to a nearby location.

Cordelia Stanwood was a pioneer wildlife photographer and naturalist, as well as a writer and craftswoman. Born in 1865, the daughter of an Ellsworth sea captain, she grew up to become a teacher and administrator in Massachusetts, Rhode Island, and Poughkeepsie, New York (where she is pictured here, age thirty-five). She eventually returned to Ellsworth where she supported herself with her wildlife photography and writing.

Miss Stanwood took this striking scene of a trio of hairy woodpeckers in the wild. Her photographs are on display at her restored Ellsworth home, part of Birdsacre, which includes the Richmond Nature Center at the Stanwood Wildlife Sanctuary.

A jack-in-the-pulpit as captured on film by "Cordy" Stanwood. More than sixty photographs from the Stanwood archives are published in the book, *Beyond the Spring: Cordelia Stanwood of Birdsacre*, by Chandler S. Richmond.

Phil Rackliffe throws some clay on a potter's wheel at Rowantrees Pottery in Blue Hill in 1947, the year he began training there under the G.I. Bill. In 1968 Rackliffe built his own kiln across town, using clay from land he and his wife Phyllis own in East Blue Hill.

Sheila Varnum has worked at Rowantrees Pottery since the 1940s. In 1976 Miss Laura Paddock (see p. 108) turned over the entire pottery business to Mrs. Varnum, who moved into the former Adelaide Pearson home on Union Street with her husband Alton and their family. The kilns are located in the rear of the homestead.

Eva Marks at work at the Rowantrees kiln, *c.* 1947. With steady hands and careful judgment, Mrs. Marks rotates the wheel at 130 revolutions a minute to fashion beautiful pottery for table use. Rowantrees pottery has found its way into homes around the world despite the insistence that art not be sacrificed to mass production.

Miss Adelaide Pearson was the mind—and the money—behind Rowantrees Pottery. The part-time Blue Hill resident, a world traveler and art patron, had the first kiln built outdoors on her property in 1934, adding others after Gandhi admonished her during a visit to India not to make a game of the ancient art of pottery making.

Miss Laura Paddock was Miss Pearson's partner at Rowantrees. Unlike Adelaide, Laura had classical training in pottery and its many and varied glazes. After arriving in Blue Hill in 1935, Miss Pearson found the clay and most of the other ingredients for her craft in the immediate area.

108

An early 1930s photograph of the Dethier brothers, attired in "plus four" golfing knickers: (from left to right) Jean, Gaston, and Edouard. Gaston was the oldest of three Belgian musician brothers and the first to come to East Blue Hill, c. 1903, from New York, where he was an organist, pianist, and composer. Edouard followed, and eventually Jean, who taught in the Blue Hill and Ellsworth school systems. Jean's son Vincent and Edouard's son Charles have been well-known Blue Hill residents.

The Foster family of Ellsworth, led by patriarch Zabud, moved there from Round Pond, Maine, c. 1860. The brothers and sisters are, from left to right: (front row) Curtis, Alwilda, James, Sarah, and Albert; (back row) Austin, John, Frank, Stetson, and Miller. Alwilda was the wife of prominent photographer Irving Osgood.

Dr. Charles C. Knowlton was a general practitioner in Ellsworth, and an elementary school is named after him. His father, John F. Knowlton, was clerk of courts for Hancock County and a law partner of Judge John Peters.

An American Legion post in Ellsworth is named in memory of Frank E. Whitmore, who died in France on April 18, 1917, while fighting in the French Foreign Legion. He was the first Ellsworth boy to give his life in World War I. The oldest son of Mr. and Mrs. Charles Whitmore, Frank graduated from Ellsworth High School in 1894.

Dr. Esther Wood was inducted into the Maine Women's Hall of Fall in 1994. The daughter of a stonecutter, Dr. Wood was born in 1905, graduated Phi Betta Kappa at Colby College in 1926, and received a Master's Degree from Radcliffe in 1929. For forty-three years she taught history at Gorham Normal School, and eventually retired to her East Blue Hill farmhouse, where she continued to write her books of local lore and a weekly newspaper column.

The son of Russian immigrants, Walter Nowick was living an isolated life as a farmer and Zen teacher when he started the Surry Opera Company in 1984. Many locals found the idea absurd, but the eclectic group of musicians soon grew, and first performed in Russia in 1986.

Mary Ellen Chase, born in Blue Hill in 1887, pursued two careers with equal skill and success—as an author and English professor at Smith College. She wrote more than thirty books of fiction, essays, biographies, and Biblical scholarships. A *Goodly Fellowship* and *Windswept* are two of her better known books, as well as her biography of Parson Jonathan Fisher. Virginia Chase Perkins, her sister, was also an author.

The aroma of molten iron and the clang, clang of his hammer were trademarks at Martin Giles' Ellsworth Falls blacksmith shop. Working from the 1920s to the 1940s, Giles' work included the shoeing of horses. The Ellsworth Historical Society museum preserves the tools of his trade just as he kept them.

Arthur Hale Parcher was a flaxen-haired pixie when he was taken to B.F. Joy's photography studio in Ellsworth to have his portrait done.

Parcher grew up to become a respected general practitioner in Ellsworth. He was a member of the Ellsworth High School Class of 1908.

Philip O'Brien's name was synonymous with the Blue Hill Fair for thirty years, when he was its secretary. Under O'Brien's leadership, fair attendance grew from 2,300 to more than 15,000. His wife, Elizabeth, bore the nickname "the secretary behind the secretary" because of her influence and hard work. (O'Brien is pictured as a young musician on p. 124.)

Small blueberry operations like the Calevan factory, located on Route 1 in Hancock, once were commonplace in Downeast Maine. Pictured are owners Cal Stinson and Evans Crabtree, with manager Roy Crabtree and some of the workers. The berries were cooked with steam in large vats, and then canned (mostly for commercial use).

Playing for the 1910 girls' basketball team at Blue Hill's George Stevens Academy were, from left to right: (front row) Olive Bettel and an unidentified player; (middle row) Belle Davidson, Mildred Bettel, and Marian Parker; (back row) Roxie Curtis, Mable Babson Mayo, and Bessie Carter.

This was the entire graduating class in 1908 of the Blue Hill Grammar School. From left to right are: (seated) Marion Dodge, Blanch Carter, and Annie Grieves; (standing) Herbert Curtis, Lester Curtis, and Carl M. Hinckley.

This portrait might have been painted, not photographed, so typical is it of the period fashions and hairstyles of Hancock County. Mary C. Davis of Lamoine proudly displays her family: (from left to right) sons Edwin, Harvey, and Vincent.

Lilla McIntyre Bowden never forgot George Stevens Academy in Blue Hill after becoming the school's valedictorian in 1904. The former school teacher, principal, and civic leader was chosen Woman of the Year by the Blue Hill Chamber of Commerce in 1981, and three years later, at age ninety-seven, was awarded the Gold Cane for being the oldest person in the community.

Varsity football was on its way out at Ellsworth High School when this photograph was taken in the fall of 1951. Those identified are: (first row, holding the ball fifth from the left) Lewis Wilson; (second row, from the left) George Stevenson (second), Jerry Kane (fourth), Kent White (fifth), and Harold "Tug" White (seventh). The coach is Edgar Turmelle.

The 1930 senior class at George Stevens Academy consisted of, from left to right: (front row) Robert Hinckley, Emery Nevells, Roy Snow, and Myron Conners; (back row) Evelyn Williams Strohmarer, Euple Owens Galbraith, Caro Leach McGraw, Dorothy Candage, and Lillian Grindle Clossen.

120

Ellsworth High School's 1925–1926 basketball team was a serious group that included, from the left: (sitting) Burton Austin (first), captain John Moore (third), Colby Foss (fourth), and Lloyd Jordan (fifth); (standing) Tommy Holmes (second), Meryle Cronkite (third), Principal Morton Whitcomb (fourth), coach Frank Stone (fifth), and Ben Whitcomb (sixth).

Basketball was popular at George Stevens Academy during the 1934–1935 season. From left to right are: (front row) Arnold McGraw, Gaylor Gray, Richard Osgood, and Daniel McGraw; (back row) Federick Cousins, Lawrence Grindle, Basil Astbury, and team manager John Osgood.

Blue Hill students also went out for baseball, such as this team photographed during the 1934–1935 season. From left to right are: (front row) Basil Astbury, Frederick Cousins, Lawrence Grindle, John Sylvester, Gaylor Gray, and Paul Duffy; (back row) Daniel McGraw, Paul Greene, Arnold McGraw, William Greene, Hubert Graham, and Richard Osgood.

The Happy Highhatters (can you find the dancing girl painted on the bass drum?) played their music in Blue Hill in the early 1930s. Pictured are, from left to right: (front row) Austin Grindle, Philip O'Brien, and Edward Clark; (back row) Frederick Grindle, Paul Saunders, and Herbert Clark.

Harold Libby (standing, at right) directed the Ellsworth High School band in the late 1940s, when his young musicians posed for this portrait. The uniforms and song selections have changed a lot since those days.

Mary Travers, Noel Paul Stookey, and Peter Yarrow—the 1960s folk trio Peter, Paul, and Mary—perform at the Blue Hill Fairgrounds in 1993. Stookey (center) and his wife Betty moved to South Blue Hill in 1974, where he converted a henhouse into a recording studio that eventually became WERU-FM, a community radio station.

Elwyn Brooks White wrote under the byline of E.B. White, but his friends called him Andy. The gifted, intensely private essayist and children's book author bought a house in Brooklin (population 600) in the early 1930s, but he and his wife Katharine didn't move in full-time until 1957. Wrote neighbor, Roy Barrette, in *Yankee* magazine after White's death in 1985, "He was my friend, and although I did not see him every day, I shall miss him because we thought alike about many things."

James Russell Wiggins was a spry eighty-nine-year-old man when he posed in the office of *The Ellsworth American* in 1992. The former *Washington Post* publisher and United Nations ambassador moved to Maine in 1969 and bought the *American*, an old New England weekly and considered by many readers to be its finest, boosting its reputation and circulation during the years that he owned it. His friendship with Brooklin neighbor E.B. White is legendary.

Acknowledgments

Although my name alone appears on the cover of this book, its preparation was not a solo performance. A symphony of individuals, libraries, and historical societies helped to make this photographic history both lively and informative. Heartfelt thanks to the following: In Ellsworth, Hale Joy made available his collection of local photographs and identified them; Herbert T. Silsby II loaned photographs and shared his knowledge; the Ellsworth Historical Society, Barbarann Foster, President, allowed the use of photographs; the Ellsworth Public Library, Patricia Foster, Library Director, loaned pictures; Stanley Richmond of Birdsacre offered material on Cordelia Stanwood. In Hancock, Sanford Phippen toured "the Point" with me, loaned fine photographs from the Hancock Historical Society, and identified them. In Surry, Carl C. Osgood contributed historical details and allowed the use of a rare collection of photographs taken by his father and grandfather. In Blue Hill, the Blue Hill Public Library, Marcia Schatz, Library Director, loaned postcard views; Sheila Varnum of Rowantrees Pottery helped with photographs and stories of the kilns; Dwight Webber turned over pictures of the Blue Hill Fair; George Stevens Academy offered portraits of alumni; the Blue Hill Historical Society, Fred Heilner, President, also helped. Special thanks to Joel White for sharing the rarely seen photograph of his father, E.B. White, and to Earle G. Shettleworth Jr. of the Maine Historic Preservation Commission for copying fine photographs, including the one on the book cover. Thanks also to Richard J. Warren, Editor and Publisher of the *Bangor Daily News*, and newspaper librarians Charles Campo and Jill Marston; and to Connee Jellison, Will Anderson, Joan Ravagnani, Sam and Helen Nyer, Wayne and Carolyn Gilreath, Barbara Rice McDade (Head Librarian, Bangor Public Library), James B. Vickery, Down East Graphics, Patricia and Carroll Pickard, Albert S. Landers, Deale Salisbury, Margaret Beardsley, Judith Leighton, Esther Wood, Walter Nowick, Alicia Anstead, Carroll Astbury, Karan Sheldon (Northeast Historic Film), Francis Hamabe, Robert H. Newall, John P. Lynch (Union Trust), and Alan Baker, Publisher of *The Ellsworth American*. Useful texts were *Hancock County, a Rock-Bound Paradise*, by Connee Jellison; *History of Ellsworth, Maine*, by Albert H. Davis; *Bits of Local History*, by William Hinckley, late columnist of *The Weekly Packet*; *Head of the Bay*, by Annie L. Clough; *A History of the Town of Hancock, 1828–1978*; and *Steamboat Lore of the Penobscot*, by John M. Richardson.

www.ingramcontent.com/pod-product-compliance
Lightning Source LLC
Chambersburg PA
CBHW050922150426
42812CB00051B/1949

* 9 7 8 1 5 3 1 6 4 0 4 3 9 *